Solomon Li was a very guarded man his entire life but discovered that writing was not just a pleasant pass time, it was also a chance for his inner thoughts and feelings to bloom. He spends most of his time practicing self-cultivation, amidst dabbling in whatever opportunities come his way.

I have already dedicated the various poems here to their respective muses, but the one person I would like to acknowledge, at last, is the hopelessly hopeful romantic I was during my 20s. Although I am now older, and a little wiser, I hope I never regret being a fool in love.

Solomon Li

JUST LAUGH

AUSTIN MACAULEY PUBLISHERS™

LONDON • CAMBRIDGE • NEW YORK • SHARJAH

Copyright © Solomon Li 2023

Ordering Information
Quantity sales: Special discounts are available on quantity purchases by corporations, associations, and others. For details, contact the publisher at the address below.

Publisher's Cataloging-in-Publication data
Li, Solomon
Just Laugh

ISBN 9781647505462 (Paperback)
ISBN 9781647505455 (Hardback)
ISBN 9781647505479 (ePub e-book)

Library of Congress Control Number: 2023904309

www.austinmacauley.com/us

First Published 2023
Austin Macauley Publishers LLC
40 Wall Street,33rd Floor, Suite 3302
New York, NY 10005
USA

mail-usa@austinmacauley.com
+1 (646) 5125767

This book was inspired by many friends who have come, gone, or stayed in my life, and they have already mostly been referenced in the poems. However, I would like to acknowledge two people who were integral to the finished product: Master Tyler, for believing in this project (and me!) from the very start, and Courtney Borrett, who has long appreciated my literary style and assisted me with unwavering dedication during the final stages.

Table of Contents

"I Can Only Laugh"

A wager's done, I've technically won, but my heart is heavy, my soul weary, my body continues nonetheless. My spirit is forced to admit it, white flag raised, that I am truly, utterly, completely done, a hallow victory's all I've won.

I can only laugh.

When challenged to feel, I did open myself, and felt, Not realizing then that it was a question of 'should,' not 'could,' Yet while I am no longer void, Cold fury flows through my veins, and I know I'll never be the same again.

For a self that can love is one that can also hate, Which I do not mind, for mine does sharpen, Whetted by clarity washing away the sleep, And I am more awake for the first time since forever.

I can only laugh.

Failed in my creed, to impart nobility, and transcendental
truths.
Despite my teachings,
Those I taught still only play the lesser game,
To win at their battles, but not at life.
When thirst for victories is quenched,
Only then will they know that they have lost,
And I will be powerless to dissuade,
Or to save them from themselves.

I can only laugh.

In accepting how I feel,
I have been subjugated to agony unimaginable,
My suffering that would be spared if I continued to deny
my heart.
Though I remain steadfast in my devotion,
I am forever shamed,
That what I felt could not reach your distant heart,
And I accept that this is fate,
Which I cannot change.

I can only laugh.

Now I am saddened,
More alone than I have ever been before,
For I can no longer pretend to be something more.
Because I have felt what it means to belong.
In despair I knew it was not meant to be,
That this could never truly be me,
Or where I belonged.

I can only laugh.

By winning a wager rigged from the start,
I've lost,
But I refuse to be defeated in defeat.
My journey shall not be in vain,
I will cling to these hurts until the end of time!

Neither will others ever influence me again,
So guarded have I become,
That while never forgotten,
I will never willingly feel again.
This I vow, as I realize how free I have become.

I can only laugh.

Courage is needed to save people from themselves. Wisdom is to accept that not everyone can be. It's harsh to accept that we have done our best, without desired results. However, while the work you have put in to others may never be finished by your hand, others can take up the mantle in your stead, much like planting a tree and knowing you will never enjoy its shade. Better instead to trust in their future than destroying those unfinished masterpieces.

When people who matter tell you not to change, it doesn't mean they wish to halt your journey. It only means that they saw a special side of you, one they hoped you would never forget. No matter how well you think you know yourself, others can help you understand it better. So when the world's taken its best shot at you, and you awaken jaded, remember that point in time when you wanted to be more, to seize the day, and be the best version of yourself. Apathy, sullenness, cruelty and isolation are the enemy. To allow those to prevail is to prepare for a descent into nothingness, for nothing cherished was ever built upon such negativity.

"Awakening from a Dream"

For years I stayed away from the games,
That pitted sharp minds against hearts of steel,
My spirit broken, my soul decayed,
Worldly wounds I resigned to never heal.

My happy days spent in peaceful lull,
Were never truly where I belonged.
Rusty sword in hand still sings as I swing,
As if yesterday, it sung when swung.

A dreaming sleep draws closer to the end,
As I finish what was once begun.

You can be measured by two things in life; your patience when you have nothing, and your attitude when you have everything. Those who can endure are those who will ensure.

An apple seed is just a seed until it is planted and becomes a tree. No matter the outcome, that was its destiny. In the same vein, whatever it is you wish to be, you already are. While you struggle so earnestly to become someone worthwhile, remember, you already have.

"A Gentleman's Heart"

I know to love is to experience loss,
No one escapes the fate of feelings.
Those prisoners for whom fear of pain deadens insides,
Their life-long suffering is quietened, not silenced.

To what rules are owed in the pursuit, the chase?
None, and I shall say this with absolute conviction,

There are no rules in love, only fools.
Compelled to play at nature's game until the last of those
who lasted can no longer endure,
Or perhaps such a prize as family is won, and that too is
but a game of love,

I speak not of the end when a comfort is given to those
who played,
Rather I address those entering such endeavors,
Uncertainly pumps through a tremulous heart
Masked by indifference, lest pride turns to shame,

There is much game to chase, desires of fire turn passions
run amok,

In moonlight the soul entwines as bodies explore within the sheets,
Whether this be the first or the fiftieth marks no such distinction,
For that is the wonder of love, and how it differs from sex.

Yet also we find the passive players, of strong feeling but weak resolve.
To love afar, and live endless romances within the realm of imagination,
That hopeful feeling their truest illumination.
Their love must never be sullied with any relationship...

Then perhaps a friendship comes along,
Which marks the beauty of one's mind and heart!
A true companion promises no more lonely days,
A promise which lasts as long as such vision endures.
Alas, it lasts not always, and thus love we abjure!

In time, we come to understand, or perhaps it is the others who do so for us,
That what we seek to call our love, is maybe curiosity, obsession, or lust?

It matters not, for someone who never played people, only the game, for each unique experience defines who we eventually become.
The joy, the hurt: the pleasures and the agony,
All mattered, then ceased to matter, then became our very matter.

A gentleman doesn't kiss and tell,
His heart is not so fickle,
A rule of the game with no rules that spells ruin for the
hopeless romantic.
To all I have loved, or been loved by in turn,
I take gratitude for those who I yearned, and those I had
spurned.

You see...

Though feelings may have changed with time,
What was felt is eternal.

Enlightenment is the ultimate affirmation of self, a supreme validation which we have all strived for since birth. It is not found in others, though it may be amongst them. Nothing about it is hidden, we simply lack the clarity to see, and that drives us insane because instinctively we know it is there, but are unable to recognize it.

Love and hatred are oft viewed as one would distinguish between good and evil. Yet as light and dark originate from the concept of sight, I tell you that they are both the same. Regardless of their various forms, clad in disguises, their panoply of masks. Both imposters may seem separate, yet it is wrong to call them indistinguishable, until such time comes that you must choose between a pleasant hatred, or a horrific love. Love and hatred are fruits that stem from the same tree. You eat what you choose to consume, yet one does not grow without the other.

"Loneliness Is"

Come one! Come All! Come gather around!

I, the host of carnal pleasures, do decree,
To my humble abode, I invite those deemed worthy.

Be ye not of the house of Ennui, come make merry, crush a
cup of wine!

Those who seem suited to dwell here are already within,
Here in my abode, betwixt fashionable vice and sin,
Be not vexed nor make complex, tonight, as we forget daily
grinds with delights.

Come one, come all! Welcome are those who drink in the
name of mirth.

What's that, are you hungry, perhaps?
Fear not, feast upon my table, glut your fill!
Here in decadence cast aside your prudences,
And witness the reason my provender is no true avenger to
the distant woes of those who mourn the empty hearth,
To be joined by those who cast aside morals for coin.
And the party goes ever on and on.

Your mortal concerns have no place in this moment, abiding realm beyond time and space.

Soon subsides artificial mirth, to remind you of your little self-worth.

It is to have come night after night after night.

Are you beginning to tire, my dearest dear friends? Perhaps you'll ask me to put this all to an end?

Nonsense!
The merriment is life, happy are we to flow in the currents of affairs not current.

Yet still my party doth diminish, my earlier guests have finished,
Their cups are full, yet they seem to think they can leave? To rest awhile, a reprieve: no one from this place ever truly leaves.
You'll return to my tables, and me, soon enough.

Fine! Go! See if we notice one less insignificant soul. For we are the hollow guests, we are the stuffed guests, lost denizens bound to this palace of plenty.

Hello, you there! Yes, you!
It is short notice, but perhaps you will come in for a drink? I offer you ambrosia, sweet release from your everyday life.

No, you are fine?
It's alright, it's alright...

I'm used to drinking alone.

"Elements of Love"

Fire scorching my very soul was never more alive prior to
this pain.
Water soothed my charred remains; it covers with cool
embrace, and threatens to drown.
Air taught me that each breath is a gift from now, to
breathe deeply is to live deeply, to live is to love.
Earth reveals the glib in me: steady, solid attraction marks
a difference to my indifference.
Metal is last, yet could be first, it is the new beginning at
the end.
I am that, to be wrought as desired, self-love is happiness
being me.

"Rhapsody in You"

(For KaHpHa)

Though you have discovered this a long time ago, I was a coward who did not wish to face your true feelings.

My admiration for you is peerless amongst our friends, for you alone combine wit and charming eccentricity with a genuine zeal for life. I confess, in my tortured private moments, I recall my clumsy dealings with your feelings, my immaturity vindicates itself.

I was able to learn that my glib and gilt is worth naught when weighed against a guilty truth. How lacking was I, occupied with a one-sided infatuation, to not realize there was someone who could inspire such pleasant feelings within.

Forgive that younger me, who has no excuses, for not seeing sooner how my actions misled and hurt your beautiful soul. Irony made me search for that one who had wounded you, and I pondered how any could treat you so? I would vent upon your behalf, a fool who did not realize that in order to find that fool, I needed to reflect: It was me, wasn't it?

So now, though our friendship is strained, and my unworthiness exposed, I only wish to unburden myself by admitting my faults. A self-absolution which would not trouble you anymore, and for that I am glad.

I do not know what would have become of us, you were never someone I could hope to equal, so I never fancied you my other half. Though I like to believe that we would have been good together while it lasted. However, good enough is never what you should settle for, never forget that!

In closing, let's have Gershwin play us another song...

Sweet Nothings

(For people like Nemo, and my ex-wife)

Has the world hurt you?
It has hurt me too, and some days, it is hard to pretend
otherwise.
Do you know why the roses have thorns?
So pretty, so fragrant, innocent, until you comprehend,
They are trying to protect themselves.
Sadly, I see that you understand that well.
Yet having thorns does not prevent them blooming into
their true selves,
Which is why, just like they,
You are beautiful.
Compare the beauty of an untarnished heart,
Innocent and pure, unmarked by trials and tribulations,
To an enduring heart,
Which continues to beat as it displays the scarry badges of
woe and suffering.
Your unfathomable heart combines the two as I've never
seen before,
And we will love with you all the more for it.

Unspoken Sentiments

(For she who taught me how to love Ghibli)

There I was, standing in the downpour of rain.

Waiting for my bus. I did not know when it would arrive, and frankly did not care. Waiting for the bus was just something to pass the time, when unexpectedly you came along, also waiting for a bus, though not mine.

We didn't say much at first: I felt strangely shy, fearing that perhaps my smile would be intimidating. But as we waited, in the rain, you offered me an umbrella...

It was the single most delightful gesture I had received for the longest time! I waited no longer, and wanted to ask your name. Can you believe that it was then that our vehicles came? Destiny has a sense of humor indeed!

"Goodbye" seemed our first greetings, yet I knew I would find you again. It was for something important, I'm sure, but what could it be? To show you my thanks? To ask your name? To return your umbrella?

No, none of those things crossed my mind when I saw you once more.

I just wanted to say,
"Hello."

In an age of increasing disbelief and emotional autonomy, we tend to place faith only in ourselves. If at all. In doing so, I hope you can make sense of who you are, and eventually realize that you are no more removed from the world than a lonely fish is removed from the ocean. Sublime awareness is found through mutual coexistence.

"The Osaka Sunset"

What assurances doth life provide?
Carpe Diem, quam minimum, credula postero.

In the land of the rising sun,
I see Osaka's sun, setting.
In twilight, I fight regrets of which I struggle in forgetting.
Neither day nor night,
I seek insights, before darkness envelops my lonely heart.

Breathe…a gentle breeze reminds me to breathe…

Long ago there lived a people who loved the sun too.
Yet love became obsession, their humanity regressed,
'Til but macabre yearnings for light was left.
Great beauty sullied by those prisoners of love who
offered their very lives,
Sun worshippers, in love with the idea of light.

I seek to understand true love
Which cannot be captured, only shared.
All fears and controlling desire,
Pale against that heavenly fire.

From where did it come? A quiet mystery.
Maybe it was always here?
Passing each day, never to stay,
and returning somewhere each night.
Her warmth my privilege, not my right.

What does it mean to hope and dream,
when you must relinquish,
One's very illumination?

It is as simple as breathing.
The air is all around us.
Respiration.
Fill your lungs, then empty...
Resist the folly of keeping it in,
What gives joyous life grows stale in your prison.

In the land of the rising sun
Twilight fades and makes way for night.
I can let go of the light, but I'll never forget,
How beautiful and bright, the Osaka sunset.

"In the Lion's Den"

(For he who would damn us all – that's right, I'm talking to YOU, Dan.)

I am he who is like the Lord, and you are one judged by Him.
So take me as your savior, your search is at an end!

The glory of the Lord is what is reflected in my very being
So do not doubt what you think you are seeing!

Unless an imitation cannot satisfy the thirst which compels you to prove yourself.
You have done enough. More than enough, though you will never be enough.

What drove you into the lion's den?
Surely it was not I?

Fake, I am not, the authentic I am not,
For I am he who is like *the Lord, but not Him.*

I could never be Him.

Despite this, you would test my faith in you, and ironically,
you do test the lord your god.

I am forced to abjure my arrogance, judged guilty, dealt
despair,
For I could not save you from yourself, though I tried.

Humility absolved humiliation, a harmony arose from the
harm I had no right to prevent,
And you had to endure your miserable and bare existence,
so that you may overcome it.

In the lion's den, you must face your fate,
Yet not alone, in that reckless abandon of life,
Alone you will fail, so together we defend,
And against the onslaught of merciless claws
You may yet make it out alive.

Even if I could not be your messiah, I am still your friend.

"Somnium Fidelus/Faithful Dream"

(For Holly, and what we could have had)

She is livid,
"You cheated on me, in my dream!"

Darling, dearest darling, I'm not to blame!
"Nonsense!" she proclaims.

Your anger, and hurt, born of each other,
Do not subside from my pleading innocence alone.
To placate that irrational side, I do have to bridge that
gap which divides our hearts,
And the fears you hold in your own.

Argument becomes louder when hearts are far away,
Our unconscious minds recognize figurative distance.

To close it, to be close to you once more,
I reveal a story I thought to not mention, until now.

A dream of other women, and my revelations.

It began, as all dreams do, in the middle, no start in sight.

All I knew was that two maidens fair, that did not resemble
you,
Came prostrate to me, and begged for my aid.

Nay, darling, let me finish!
Stay your open hand,
'Til I am done with this story I would not tell, unless I had
a motive to sell.

The two maidens explained their plight, and promised me
all manner of delights,
If I rescued their princess, who was beautiful as the stars,
lovelier than any flower,
A goddess whose charm made the heavens forlorn with
longing.
A future queen whose end would doom their kind,
For she was the only sovereign worthy of the throne.

A brave hero such as I could not refuse their earnest
requests,
Together they led me to the den where a draconian
monster lies in wait
I vaguely recall it, for the monster was defeated, before I
even knew it.
Such is the nature of a dream, for it is no nightmare.
And this nightly vision was of pretty women.

Victorious was I, and I knew my prize,
For this princess was saved, she and her handmaidens
reunited,

As I escort them back to their lands, the princess offers me
her hand.
Her look is coy and sly,
As she prepared to bathe by the scenic lake
Showing me, that neither she, nor her maidens, were shy.

And perhaps in my younger days I would have played,
Frolicking in the waters with such lithe and buxom vixens,
To enjoy their company, and join in their fun,
Was an offer that would tempt anyone!

Yet at that moment I was overcome by a different part of
me,
One less impressed with the shapely bodies and pretty
faces,
Or such carnal pleasures of that would ensue
For in that moment, I thought of you.

It was early in our relationship; I did not know you well,
Yet what fledgling bonds we had forged was enough for
me to tell,
That I would not be swayed by physical desires,
I aimed to be true to you,
True to the idea of love.

We are traveling by the roadside now, and a new respect I
sense,
From my female companions, whose bodies I did not claim
in recompense
Especially the princess, with whom I held hands,
As a friendly and gentlemanly sign, it was innocent.

"Why"? She asked me as I returned them to their castle,
Could it bet I did not care for their allure?
I sigh, longingly, for their bodies were not yet dry from the lake,
And as cloth hung to bodies, I pondered, my mistake?

"My fair ladies, I am not the best of men. Yet I do have a sweetheart, far better than I deserve. We are not oft in each other's presence, and I am unsure if I what I feel is rightly considered love.
Regardless, she is one worthy of my full attention, in a different way to what I feel for you three.
I cannot bring myself to dishonor her,
Her sadness would break my heart."

These ladies smile, understandingly, and the future queen bestows a kiss upon my cheek,
Which I return, as I bow, to her delicate and gentle hand, before I awoke.

A dream? Just a dream, yet perturbing as revelation.
Had I been tested, and if so, did I succeed?

What proof or assurance can I provide,
In order for your suspicions to subside?

I only know, that though I was unfaithful in your dreams,
For me to agree to infidelity is unknown,
Even in my own.

~She Stumbles in Charm~

"I never learned how to breathe through my mouth, and I've got a cold – stop laughing at me!"

(Inspired by Lord Byron, dedicated to Courtney, the only person I know who's younger than me, yet appreciates classical literature.)

She stumbles in charm, pensive and glad,
Endearingly dumb, so cute when she's mad,
For all that she sees, and discounts the lies,
A young lady who's 'full,' yet still enjoys fries,
She's a lovely painting of simpler times gone by.

One moment she is here, the next she is gone,
Her sunshine-locks vibrant in cascade flow,
Such child-like manners enhance jubilant fun,
Her eyes wear a smile laced with mischief-glow.
Unaware, voluptuous and fair, softly bemoans, "How tragic and sad!"
She laments that Jeff Goldblum is not her dad.
Such innocence far from mere vapidness, perhaps hinting some secret happiness?

So at last, as moonlight zenith serenades the darkened
skies,
She curls and huddles,
Tender yawns,
Self-cuddles,
At peace with her day lived, another day earned,
Drifts away, satisfied, with all she has learnt.

"Gladiator Rex: The Empathetic Nihilist"

(For Oscar, the stoic of my peers)

A roar from the crowds draws me in
To the bloody amusements of the coliseum.
As I watch them maim, I consider,
What true reasons drew me hither?

Perhaps the simple savagery of our natures,
Is why carnage spilled grants the audience such delight.
Yet my fetish is not from the sight of muscled limbs
cleaving flesh from bone,
It lies in the champion's eyes.

Those dark orbs void of hope, yet resonate with yearning
for a human connection.
At perhaps one more humane than human.

His name was Spear, the king of all warriors!
Fearless, without peer,
A man who knew of no other life than the daily
diminishment of others.
By day he trained with men, to fight!
Bedding countless women at night.

Each meal a feast, he dines on the glory of each victory,
Tomorrow never comes, for today is his reign!
Burning brighter than the stars, roaring louder than thunder,
Until what satisfied him ceased to, his thoughts did wander.

His self-worth was bound to others, as a castle built on sand.
His legacy was forgotten as an emptiness grew within.
One which would not subside no matter how much blood was spilled.
No matter how many women,
No matter what kinds of food.
He knew that he was only known for one thing: killing.
It was his very existence, the key word being 'was.'

No longer fulfilled by pleasing the crowds,
Spear asked what was the meaning of it all?
He had become an empathetic nihilist.
A torturous state that speaks of feelings unresolved.

Despair takes many forms, often with irony in mind.
It is the ultimate comeuppance, the truest measure of our miserable existence.
Spear did not weaken, his soul was not broken,
But the darkness made him human only in token.
Gladiator Rex had become a monstrous god of carnage.
That was what the crowds whispered, though they always came to watch.
Fascinated by the brutal artistry he employed,

41

They always cheered, though it made them question as
Spear once did,
Why were they here?

All this I saw, and witnessing their shame,
In realizing how differences still make us the same.
We were the victor, and the victim, the predator, and the
prey.

I requested to see Spear, to sate these curiosities I
contained.
His stable is a palace, and I dine at his table,
Though he motions the act of eating, there is no culinary
delight.
We do not speak, at first, but I am surprised to find,
That sharp was his skill, yet so was his mind!

It was withdrawn: the blood lusting eyes which glowed
with desperation
To try and find meaning in his unique affliction.
It was not the Spear I had known:
It was one that had grown weary of the crowd's adoration,
and sought reprieve from that alienation.

We discuss many things, and I discover that politics is his
favorite to discuss.
He is a simple man, and looks at cowardice with disgust.
I ask him if he ever feared death, and he denied such
aversion to blissful release once enveloped in eternal
sleep.
So I asked him what it was that he lived for?

That question brought the darkness forth,
And though my fascination took no heed of my senses,
I reveal the truth that he dared not face.

A victorious coward only hides the truth, with nothing to
live for, no one to love,
That type of life is not enough.

He approaches me, and I do not tremble, for I am always
seeing his eyes, those windows of a soul which pleads for
peace, yet housed within a mind and body that knows no
other living.

"What must I do?"

I tell him what I have always thought of him, that he was
Spear, the king of Coliseums!
There were crowds from afar that traveled to come see
him.

Yet his bloody reign was not the sport of a champion, but a
beast, less than a man.
Our humanity contained a savage nature, yet tempered by
the nobility of our potential.
We talk, and I uttered words of the philosophical masters,
What nearly conquered him, what he sought to quell,
Was the absence of connections, an existential Hell.

It is time for me to leave, though we make a vow, that I
would see my new friend's next fight.
And what I saw restored the faith, a majestic sight.

He was praised before, and mentioned with admiration,
Yet today he received the crowd's full adoration!
Rather than a macabre scene
All challengers he met with magnanimity befitting a true
king,

Those worthy he defeated,
And spared, to fight another day
Those not, were graced by the song of his blade.
In doing so he delighted the crowds who saw him with
more dimensions than ever before!

This was what I saw, who I had seen before.

And as usual it is his eyes where I fix my gaze,
He was human again, with hope and purpose in each
motion, not a vengeful shade that sought to devour a world
he had yet to understand.
His spirit once a desolate well, now a thriving river,
He was doing what he did best.
My friend was back, and better than ever
The invincible Spear, Gladiator Rex.

"Rock Paper Scissors"

The game is simple enough

Rock beats scissors.
Scissors beats paper.
Paper beats rock.

So simple to imagine, what could be,
Were it not for infighting that occupies these three.

Such is how the game of love is played.

I'm vulnerable, hurting, resolved to be unfeeling.
I accept the loss, unable to believe how I could ever be
loved.

Such is the game of love

Acceptance negates vulnerability.
Faith validates your pain
Open love bests apathy

The game is simple enough, even if the players are not.

Nihilism is not original; it serves no purpose except a premature end. Reality is not a nightmare any more than it is a dream. It is our inherent quest to define good and evil we forget that existence does not care for such trivialities. Rather, the real good does not need you to proclaim it, the true evil lies in the song never sung those works never finished, and the abandoned nexus. What rule prevents dreams from becoming reality, just because they are dreams? No rule, only the dreamer.

"Red Flower District"

I once owned a rose bush, and tried to make it grow.
Yet though my plant was once in full bloom,
Soon, no flowers grew, all efforts in vain.
The petals withered, and I knew such was my fate
So I abandoned the plant,
Resigned to be Alone.

I now just buy roses, when I needed them.
Problem solved!

The florist bouquet temporarily eases my dejection.
Except, each rose soon wilts and dies.
Leaving me alone once more.

Why am I surprised?
Eventually, do not all roses do the same?

Soon I stopped renting them, and returned to my garden.
I tend my little plant patiently, unlike before,
There is no need to rush.
And soon, a little rose bud sprouts,
Along with it, my heart bloomed.

A single rose that came from my care, is worth a hundred bought.
It was never the flowers but affirmation I sought.

I think about the people I knew, and I wonder if they were real. Especially those who I came to feel strongly for. Always, I've considered, who was she to me? Maybe nothing more than a dream, a vision, or a song given human form. Perhaps even a goddess visiting from another realm. I've come to realize that it doesn't matter. If you think about them, and draw strength from your memories that feature them, it's real to you. At the end of the day, what's more important: Proving that they existed, or living like they never stopped being a part of your life?

"The Three Fatal
Ls of Attraction"

There is like, there is lust, and there is love.

When I am in like with you,
It is so easy to tell
For our friendship is an ideal spell
There is just a sense of belonging,
The same that can be shared by anyone
Except you're not just anyone.
Not to me.

When I am in lust with you
Be prepared for flirty fun!
Who I was, and who I want to be
Are blurred as we become both more and less than friends,
No matter which one is the hunter,
We both enjoy the chase,
Thrills born of such exquisite taste.
While passion rules the stage,
We explore each other as never before.

When I am in love with you,
It can be difficult to reveal

For we are old souls reunited from a past life.
*I **know** you,*
Though I cannot recall your previous name.
Perhaps that is why I fell in love,
Why things will never be the same.
Two halves are joined, and it would seem a crime
If we were not still joined for the rest of time.
I know this feeling to be true,
The World stays still when I am with you.

These three are deadly, not in and of themselves,
But because human cannot tell apart the sisters,
Charming with multiple delights,
Until you make the mistake of thinking one is another.

Needless suffering is your station,
If you liked them only for their face.
To mistake your lust or like for love
Suffer agony of feelings misplaced.

Then there is always regret,
When love is mistaken for lust, or merely like.
For you bear witness to a tragedy written by your own
hand,
As they give theirs to another who has seen,
The gift that is their being,
Leaving you to ponder what could have been.

Confusion lies in wait,
For those who think that their like is more akin to love or
lust,

Heavier feelings which undermine the simple pleasures
Of someone who already gives you affection.
And the truth is revealed, that you yourself are unfulfilled,
Not the person in question.

Verily I remind us that no poison or blade can harm others
more than how you treat them,
For when you are ignorant of your true feelings even a
kiss can kill.

"Daughters of Shanghai"

*(For Kublai Khan, the poem by Samuel Taylor Coleridge.
Similarly, I also fashioned this from a fever dream I
experienced during one particularly stifling summer
night.)*

Amidst an oriental land,
A city reformed by necessity,
As East and West collide,
To assume respective dignities.

Such fragrance! Sounds! The sights!
Purveyors of all manner of exotic delights,
Offer the hope of respite, for home grown locals and
tourists alike.

The tourist joints are wonders to behold,
A plethora of performances, and products sold.
Should you deign to rest there a while,
You will know this enchanting city fit to be a sovereign's
pleasure garden.

Yet it is not in the hustling bustling cadence of market
streets,

Where a fabled treasure is hidden.
The true intricacies of Shanghai lie in what is known to few:
The Jade Tea House of Madam Yu.

Now your curiosity is piqued, and has yet to peak,
For no book or map may serve as guide.
Invitation alone serves as lock, and key.
Should fortune smile, and should it be your fate,
Your longing you may yet placate.

Pay close attention!
Not to inlaid pearl or such jeweled exteriors
Nor beautiful maidens who occupy the interiors.
Nay, as we pass gates that seemingly hold back modern times themselves,
Displaced senses adjust to the setting now beheld.
And you will be greeted with Madam Yu.

She is less a matron, than a dowager.
One whose power radiates in absences,
For she is our host, and we the guest,
As we take the chance to take splendid rest.

Each time our tea cup is refilled a new girl replaces the last,
I marvel at how each brew could speak of flavors renewed,
That I could barely comprehend.

She informs me, when I ask, that the greatest treasure here
can be expressed by one relic: a dainty pair of glass
slippers, forged from the finest Chinese crystal.

I must admit that I was confused,
For while these were fashioned from luxury material,
Yet rather than transparency, a veined inlay has spread,
In these crystal footwear with gold and silver spider web.

Madam Yu explains,
"It is a tradition, for all the maidens,
Upon reaching mastery of such skills as we offer,
Will wear these and prove themselves with 10,000 paces.
This will determine their place.
Once broken, they are repaired with the finest precious
metals,
To be used for the next girl, the next test."

I was stunned, for surely it was impossible?
She assured me that nothing was impossible, with the right
mindset.

"In the journey of 10,000 steps, it is the glass shoe that
breaks,
But the worthy do not bend under such torture."

My shocking realization is apparent,
The shoes need not be intact to pass this final challenge,
Only the spirit of those who wore them.

The rest of my time was spent drinking tea, in silence.

For I realize now, how difficult to see at first glance,
Atrocities committed, endured and imagined,
Have not ruined the brews I sampled with new found
respect.
A new perspective, once tasted, I'll never forget.

"The Existential Rhetoric"

In choosing love, we choose to be vulnerable, a choice that essentially means choosing to be hurt by the right person.

In this day and age, my peers have opted to dissect this process, where control of such feelings are expressed with merely the concept of one's interest.

I wonder then, if it were not easier, and more interesting, to fall in love with an idea, the ideal aspects of any romantic candidate. Could there not be more meaning in a worthy simulation, than a harsh truth?

I confess, in my case, my truest friends are obtained by comrades since expired, or who never physically were. Our interactions are held in high confidence, with opinions less frequently mired.

So unto that same logic holds sway,
A loving companion to the end of days,
Could then not, in competitions vie,
Artificial receptacles of affection qualify?

Imagine, a limitless position with any persons I could envision! Dining with Caesar, symposiums with great thinkers, and poems dedicated to the rarest beauties sought near and far...

My every moment is a retreat from an unfeeling world, to consort with the most delightful and admirable alike.

Yet once more, when the pages are turned, the volume closed, I am forced to put my mind to the solitude, the ennui of my soul. Vanity convinces me that I do not need real human connections, yet it is suffering which best allows me to connect.

Could this be why the divine remain silent? As a reminder that omnipotence can boast little power against inadequacies, such as those faced when exploring the human condition.

Or perhaps this stems not from the options of loving another, yet a self-love that we seek to fill, and once achieved, will allow us to forgive society's imperfections. Whatever the reason, I do exist, right here, and now, and given time, I no longer think I am so different.

If we criticize others for flaws they are trying to overcome, are you a hypocrite?

When we die of natural causes one's very biology betrays us through integral design. To live is therefore a prolonged form of unwitting suicide. If given the option to extend it, and we do not take it, would it be a conscious one? If I accept, does immortality means I stopped death, or gained new life?

I cannot know what I am supposed to believe in order to understand my existence.

I can accept that I am not able to understand everything about my existence.

I can know more about myself over time; it allows me to better believe in my own existence.

"All That Glitters Is Gold"

*(In honor of Captain Goldie, a personage whom I hold in
greatest esteem, for your diplomacy and genuine
Goodness.)*

How learned, how educated, how refined indeed!
Such views of enviable scholars,
Meting good advice and integrity alike in social
ecosystems centered on likes.

If only we unenlightened could consider,
Their manner, with which we could deliver,
Respectable values and morals held dear,
To reflect upon deepest, private, fears.

A wise man once said: fish given was fish eaten in a day,
Learning to fish would keep the hunger at bay.
That same wise man spends time in deep contemplation,
Complete by sagely bliss.
Unaware that such tedium makes him no better than a fish.
For if it is instinct for a fish to swim,
A sage giving wisdom is exactly what we'd expect of him.

How unoriginal, how uninspired!

Taking wisdom from others requires a measure of our own.

The question of 'why' is itself the truest mark of intellect,
Discourse and schooling notwithstanding,
Ours becomes yours with a simple 'Y.'

Should we know one thing, and one thing only,
Knowing that we cannot know is wisdom in its entirety.
Plato could have been his own master as much as Socrates,
Yet chose to credit the latter instead, to avoid the strife,
In thinking the same thinking, that took his teacher's life.

All that glitters is gold for those who know no better.
Which is all of us, when our purpose stays unclear,
Yet with willing minds and open hearts,
Can come to accept what we once could not.

Given the choice between potential lovers, I would choose myself. There can be no surer love than self-respect, no deeper affection than kindness, and no better outcome than avoiding hurt. That is what I know, yet I will speak for what I don't, which is larger. Being human is to know the logical path, yet follow the passionate one. It is one of the things that makes life so interesting, and even, perhaps, makes us wiser in the long run.

"Swan Song"

For the world to share in my fragile grasp of existence,
The only sincere gesture I can offer
The only thing I can say is:
Thank you for the feelings.

"Ave Potato Maria"

(In sooth, my first love)

"If my true love does not exist,
Then I am at a loss for words.
For is there greater bliss than this?
A perfect bowl of humble roots,
That take root in thine heart and soul,
A golden array, angelick panoply,
That speaks not nor gives hint of nightshade kin, despoils
thy name.
For a Potato by any other, is still as wholesome as thou.
Modest is the pure white soul,
So satisfying, your coy shell is breached,
Each time a rapturous symphony,
My tongue envelopes the savory-sweet.
And as all passions do belie, I say just one more, one
more, until another has gone by.
Not more, nor less, the hint of shame so ameliorates each
escapade.
You are my Adonis, my Helen, my Achilles tendon...
If this yearning burn is the price of each kiss,
My broken heart be set aflame once again,
As the dewdrop salt fused with sublime sheen,
True love lives on in the timeless senses,

This sight, this scent, the taste divine,
How you've always been there,
Oh truest love of mine."

"My Hamburger Venus"

(For the Border Burger of Namesake's Village)

"Tis our wedding night,
My lady, she awaits,
Postures, posturing, her auburn hair,
Patient and still,
Still, more lovely, more fair,
Than that I had once envisioned.
For I make no move to her, merely watching her,
Drinking in her charm, her allure,
She is Venus in mortal form.
Her silence is beckoning,
Her anxious heart beats beetroot red,
Cascading fresh fielded tresses,
That inlaid trim of Spanish scarlet,
The hem and sew of her emerald dress.
So much so that my heart be still,
And breathless, ever so.
How delicate her complexion,
Yet no hint of weakness,
The lace that binds her bosom deep,
Delivers my bride with single, poignant, sweep.
Accompanied by dowry of caskets gold,
Worth their salt, but true worth untold,

Is my maiden, who remains a maiden still,
On the snowy bedsheets she awaits.
Tenderly, carefully, I make my embrace.
As my first bite drawn blood that marks her, forever
changed, then devoured, by fervor of all our senses!
How she nourishes me, and strengthens,
Emboldens me, as time lengthens.
And I am content with the World.
The path to a man's heart is oft thought though his
stomach-
Quenched and sated, my affection deepens,
For this meal was a meal made with love."

My dates: "So what exactly does a Romantic poet do?"

Me: "Basically, I imagine making out with my meals."

My dates: "... Wow... you really like food, don't you?"

Me: "Well yeah, but, I mean, not more than anyone else, right?"

My Dates: "Are you depressed? It's cool if you are, we can talk about it if you want?"

Me:...

My Dates: "Or, maybe, we could just keep ordering?"

Me: Thank you, that would be nice.

"Foul Infidelity"

(Also for Holly, who reminded me to drink more water, and eat less fried food… But what is a long life without enjoyment?)

My darling, forgive me?
I am a man, and men have needs.

Please, try to consider, that I am but a mortal man.
Not made of stone but prone to persuasions of the flesh,
As are the rest of human kind.

I did stray, and erred, for despite my ideals I hunger for
primal satisfaction absent in our otherwise happy lives.

Resorting to lies to avoid hurting you,
Conspiring to conceal that darkest truth of my deception.

At first, how simple and small,
My slip was just a slip, not a fall.
So no need to tell you,
My pangs of conscience assuaged that a one-time
occurrence, never to be repeated, would strengthen our
love into something more deep seated.

Thus, was it not a good thing?
For us, I mean.
To have infidelity draw us closer, not apart.
To deny my passions is to cleave the longings of my mortal heart.
Though yearning for your approval, while drawn to that forbidden desire.

Did you ever suspect?
Was your trust implicit?

My mistress's scent disguised, to mask my shame with it.
In truth, each time we kissed I feared,
That you would taste the sin upon my lips.
And when you asked me what was wrong as I pulled away,
I knew that wedge would stubbornly persist in driving away the best part of my life.
You, darling dearest, you...

Maybe it was my fault then, when I happened to witness a karmic retribution.
That now you were cheating on our sacred covenant too.

My first though, relief, for now she who is with sin cannot cast the first stone.
Yet I could only watch in shock as you enjoyed yourself as I have never seen before.
How could you?!
Feigning innocence later, yet you cannot fool me!

*And to my further bewilderment, that clown was not your
only lover,
You went to another, and I saw you throw away any
composure,
As you gave way to the pleasure that your body so craved.
You were treated like a queen, I suppose.*

*That night you return, I am waiting.
You decline dinner, and the atmosphere is tense.
Stillness broken, as I break the silence.*

*"I saw you today. You broke our promise to be true."
In defense, she exclaims, "You cheated on me too!"
She had known for a while now, despite my guile, for a
woman knows these things.*

*I do not deny it, and I confess, "Yes,"
As I recount how I could not resist those legs,
and as I buried my teeth into those breasts, I admit I forgot
about my darling entirely.*

*Then she breaks down as the truth unfolds, a flood of
relief, a desperate desire to unburden her guilt, as well as
a small ray of hope that we could move past this.
She spares me no detail, about how she had wanted it so
badly, and of all the different combinations she tried,
which made her feel sick afterwards, yet she couldn't stop.*

*I hold her, she returns my embrace, and now we cup each
other's face.*

I whisper to her my regret, and she reveals to me,
That the secrecy hurt her more than the act,
My infidelity was worsened by that fact.

How strange, for we both now laugh, and cannot stop our laughter,
This could be the closeness we were after.

"I'm sorry."
"I'm sorry too."

I promise her that I will always tell her if I strayed from our healthy diet,
if I cheated on her with fried chicken.
And she promises that McDonalds nor Burger King could never replace my cooking.

Now, with all the secrecy of our affairs revealed, I wonder,
Could other couples relate to my case of infidelity most fowl?
Perhaps honesty is the best policy after all.

"愛 / Ai"

(For Jake, who gets his own novel in 'Osaka Sunrise')

Dearest disciple,

It pains me to hear of your now desolate soul, deprived of light, that you must suffer too a love unrequited. Yet I implore you to hear me, that my words might reach you in the dark of your self-imposed emotional exile.

It hurts…
It hurts so badly that you could just die.
I know, I understand…

But please, you should not stop feeling just yet,

Because,

Love is essential, to master anything in life.

Mastery is greatness, and you cannot become great if you do not get involved, and you cannot understand just how involved you can be without experiencing what it means to love.

It hurts at the time, like falling, and then the fall, yet who chooses to crawl forever?

We all should seek to stand on our own feet.

Even if we must do so alone.

Did I not teach you? With an open heart, we are never truly alone.

So, when you become so wise that you can win your battles without the need to fight,

You may have learned how to love without needing to suffer.

At which time, you will become the master, and I your willing student.

Please take care of yourself.

With all my esteem,

'Shifu.'

"No Chill"

My phone vibrates, I see a flashing light.
A small thrill rushes in unbridled delight.
Which came first?
The light I saw, the buzz emitted,
Or perhaps, it was my heart on edge this entire time.
Waiting for you to respond, and continue our game of
virtual tag.

And the strangest thoughts do cross my mind,
As we chat away at mundanities which offer only a
glimpse of our daily lives.
To feel our connection build as conversation transcends
distance.
Comfortable are we, engaged in the randomness of being
ourselves.
A natural delight I sought, then found, as we lay the
foundations of a long-distance bond.

Then you stopped, and I was forced to stop, too.

One sided conversations do not offer much attraction as I
press send and am replied with "message seen."

Now forced to dam my damned elation, what once flowed
so freely, a sign I was, maybe, enjoying myself too much.

More than you…

Or it could be, as my darkest thoughts manifest, that the
hidden meaning is that there is none.
I was simply a way to pass the time…

I could never forget, however I pretended, that we live
lives distanced by oceans and lands spanning the planet
itself,
Even so, that fact is meaningless as we indulged within
our private world.

I have to ask myself, what do you want from me?
For each time I think we grow to know the other better,
Cold silence is something that upsets the melody.

My greatest fear is I have offended you,
Second only to I care too much.
In seeking to deliver responses which are fresh, not frozen,
My charade of coolness exposes how I have no chill.

What can I do, but suffer in silence, meditating on the
matter,
Allowing ill passions to run their course.
And the next time you message, I am surprised to find,
How overjoyed I am to see your name,
Brightening the screen, in much the same, you brighten my
spirits.

"Faith at the Bottom of a Well"

(For Ben, in hopes that's you will find your ikigai)

The Umbral Solaris, twin of day,
Graces evening skies with shade of evening gray,
So as I do hope to find my answer, once pondering 'neath,
A spirit wanes in contrast to faith unsheathed.

As the Moon does wax and wane,
In towards my soul shall I try escape,
This horror of an unfelt pain,
To exist rather than to live,
Taking more than myself can give,
And any transient epiphany gained is soon lost as my
conviction is too weak and bleak to hold that divine love,
that unfelt embrace.
Yet I persevere, because I believe.

To my left are the values I was taught,
To the right, conscience recognizes wrong from right,
But I, uncentered, am placed in the center of the moral
war,
Fought and won,
Only to be undone,
Thus infighting continues ever on...

Unless!
Unless that faith, shaken yet not yet broken,
Can begin to heal the tenuous rifts in between a fragile
bridge of doctrine,
Nexus to a phobia, that I alone must be held responsible
for an entire flock of sheep.

Can a silent shepherd can still be heard?

Though unsure, that what I see from my limited view can
be considered the Sun,
I know instead of condemning the unknown,
I can venture past the darkness towards a glimmering
light,
And I will determine, for myself,
Amidst ancient wisdom and axioms anachronistic,
Which facts are in fact the vindicated truth.

And though the preachers claim that the sky is only as
high as the length of this well,
I shall venture forth, and discover for myself, the limits of
Heaven and Earth.

"An Impossible Dream"

They told the rat he could never be a butterfly, but he did not listen to the naysayers nor those who doubted. The rat continued to believe in such dreams that one day would reach through the divide of the sleeping and the waking world.

And that's how we got bats.

"Going Their Own Way"

We are all sinful creatures.

I lie wake each night, while the shadows envelop light,
To ponder if what higher power that might exist,
Indeed take pleasure in our suffering plights.
I do not doubt our pleas fall on deaf ears.

We are all pitiful beings, I cannot deny.
If you love me for who I am, is that not a reason to die?
What I am is fleeting,
There may come a day you fall back, retreating,
From the temporary me that stands before you.

That is the summation of their false divinity, no matter
how warm and humane it appears. All interaction merely a
curiosity, experiments to abandon when bored. That is
how an alien amusement expresses the semblance of love,
and though human flesh may they take, to make a bond
that promises all, you will discover that such soulless
shameless beings do exist.

Beyond angels and demons, we are more so than either,
And more well suited to self damnation.

Those who crave a god so, as to worship any Idol they might find.
This is our destiny, and your salvation, once found.

Human Calculus

(For Maddie the Sleuther)

We all know the basic math of life, where 1 and 1 make 2.
Then there is another truth, in love,
Where numbers take value, subject to the mathematician's
view,
And when 1 and 1 make more than 2,
That is to say, 'we' are greater than just me + you.

Did you know?
There's an entire universe in the numbers, a study spans
galaxies within that theoretical world.
Much the same way we find a numerical consistency
present in our own.
From golden ratios to variational trends, the presence of
mathematics in the living world is intrinsic to our being.
No matter what language spoken or written, mathematics
is always the same. In this vein, it represents something
that can be described as truth.

So what then of emotions, and how are they expressed?
Surely a quandary that quadratics don't address...do
they?

*If it is relationships you seek, the cartesian plane will
explain,*
*In simple terms, for complexities of words and feelings
hold no sway to the simple brilliance here.*
*There are intersecting lines, which represent the people
we meet, who came and went.*
*Then consider parallel lines that stay in range, a
possibility that proximities of what if, but never to be…*
*Then there are those relationships of asymptotes, to seek a
meaning from the world itself, seeking to reach the axis of
fundamental truth.*

*In all that computational data, I might grow easier to let
elation slide,*
*The admiration of a metaphysical world that allows for all
denotation.*
*So perhaps one day, you begin to grow distance, a
dispassionate visitor in this place.*
Where you may see possibilities, yet never a face.

*If so, I will tell you a tale of my friend, a wiser girl of
lively passion and zest,*
Compassionate and kind to all people she met.
Her example was what helped me pass this test,
One of alienation from and for the mind's perception.
*Her warm heart amidst the numbers, neither cold nor
unfeeling,*

Revealed how easy it is to forget,
It was reducing things down to just a number that led to
my regrets.

Wiser now, I can admit, I'm but a student of Human
calculus!

Excuses: A Trilogy of Tremulous Feelings

(For those who wished, but realized it would never be.)

"I Like You, but – Part 1/3"

"Whenever I'm out with her, everybody calls me sir"
I like it when we stroll through the streets,
And you take my arm, linked with yours,
A beautiful lady, and I, playing the gentleman.
With you by my side l am a taller and more handsome
man, chest puffed and brimming with pride,
Betraying my grateful heart inside.

I like it when we go out for meals,
Where the waiters steal glances as we wait,
As if to say how envious they are of we,
When you smile at my antics that tell of all we have shared
in the years past, and will in years to come.
Finally, the food arrives, but we take no notice of each and
every sumptuous dish,
Good company is the secret to fine dining.

I like it when my friends complain,
That they could not find others that could compare,

To you, and all your grace and wit and charm,
Paired with the allure of your goddess face,
Luscious hair that flows as a velveteen river,
My friends keep urging, "Just go out with her!"

I like it when we spend time alone,
Our conversations breathe warmth in towards my soul,
and that warmth then does spread to all my limbs.
As my fingers brush away the fringe which hides your
gorgeous eyes,
As before I am aware we have embraced,
Your head now resting against my nape,
As we stay still and breathe the same air, within the same
space and time as one another.
Sharing a moment of possibilities.
Perhaps we are waiting for the first move,
For our lips to silently reveal what we choose.
Yet mine never do.
And disappointment is tactfully hidden,
As you say, "It's late," and I agree, and I do as bidden,
I leave before doing something I'll regret.

I like you, but this isn't 'love.' It's the romance of a
friendship too dear for me to gamble on a night of
amorous fun.
And though I do not doubt that as couples we could be so
much more,
It's something we'll likely never become.

Instead, I give you something that belies the playfulness I
always use to survive,

These dangerous and uncharted waters known as dating in
the modern age.
That no matter who you see and choose to be with,
I will always treasure that bond between us,
Uncomplicated by what might have been.

"I Want You, but – Part2/3"

I am not a man so callous as to play with a lady's heart,
Though when the mood is right,
I play with her body, focused as a potter sculpts clay.

My fingers caress, they cup each curve,
Trace the circuitry of her body,
Giving way to my touch,
Her mind is still as tranquil state defines the closeness of
skin-to-skin embrace.

We talk, as men and women do, with our words,
And with our mood in flux,
When conversation lulls to whispers uttered,
When clothing melts away, a lowering of walls,
A slow burning akin to concupiscent drawl,

There is a connection made, fanned by the flames of
nonverbal signals flowing freely,
As you relax while I do my thing,
Though as stupor gives way to your stark realization,
That I have stalled my hands, halted our escalation,
Our musical harmony which silently played,
That silence becomes silent as intentions seem delayed.

You sense my hesitations, they attract your reservations,
So we do not finish that dance we had begun to dance
today.

I want you, true, but I understand the truth,
You don't trust me enough to want me too.
And I don't blame you for it.
I think of you as wiser for it.
As friends we should not do something we might regret.

"I Love You, but – Part 3/3"

Unlike before, when I'm invited to your place,
We do not sit side to side, instead, face to face.
Distance spanning what has become of our emotional
space.

A healthy attraction requires not that things go right,
Instead, they rely on nothing going wrong.
You reveal to me of your sleepless nights,
Among many a thought, oh, how vulnerable you've
become,
When I asked you, "Be mine!"
And I would be yours.

All shared feelings are a gamble,
We might win, we may lose.
To go all in is a statement,
To accept whatever they choose.

As for I, for all my ambivalent intentions,
Have sincerely broached this topic with you,
That we could build something strong, something lasting,
But though I'm far better than all the others,
Am I still not good enough for you?

A few words are exchanged,
But we know what has been said,
Are all the words we need to spare,
For a friendship that will soon be dead.

A sullenness replaces joy which we carried in our hearts,
We are now less completed beings; we are now just the
sum of all our parts.
But we depart in peace, too mature to fall for games of
blame,
Only relieved, as the jaded are, that we avoided singes
from these flames.

As for I, who am disappointed, true,
Angry that this is how things must be, it is not an
animosity for you.
Afterall, don't you know by now?
I love you, enough to express my feelings true.
I love you, but we perhaps we realized, deep down,
*I am not **in** love with you.*

"Farewell My King"

(For Chris O-sama, who taught me all I know about basketball and other national sports. It was my privilege to serve you on the South-Eastern front.)

"In my entire life filled by pleasure and strife,
My heart has been broken only twice,
The first was when he married his wife,
The second, when he would leave to start a new life.

Certainly, my sentiments are echoed by all our peers,
We will create fond memories, instead of bitter tears.
Let the dice roll, however they may land,
And celebrate good times with Yakuman hands!

Though, before you go, I would unlay all that I have long
wished to artfully reveal the esteem which I have for you,
only to decide the time was never right.

It is almost not prudent to say,
What I feel for you, it is an upmost respect,
Dare I say even, admiration?
For you are and have always continued to be yourself,
Unconcerned by petty adulation.

Indeed, you are the Man who many strive to be.

In your youth, a prudent lad,
A clever boy who rarely got mad.
In your prime, an outstanding gentleman!
Walked with kings, nor lose the common touch,
You were a people's man, but not overly much,
I witness you display your golden soul time and time
again!
No doubt when you grow older, and maybe rounder,
You will venerate that wisdom even sounder,
A Laconic King matched by an Amazon Queen,
I bless you and all yours until the very end of your days!"

To Destroy Man

(In tribute to Rod Serling and "The Twilight Zone")

I like you as a friend.

"But I love you."

You're like a brother to me.

"But I love you!"

I don't want to ruin our friendship.

"But I love you…"

Another response each confessor dreads hearing: "Awww, thank you!"

The lovestruck individual, who falls in love only to find that the price was not his heart, but self-worth. A phenomenon so warped that only in the real world do people use companionship as a stepping stone for intimate relations. Such tragedies are common, for denizens trapped in "The Friend Zone."

"Osaka Moonlight"

She was cool, she was soothing,
She was still gentle-bright,
I've known her on vibrant sunny days,
I loved her best, when it was just us, at night,
Strolling about the Osaka moonlight.

There was no goal, no destination, and for once I held no
reservations.
As I held on to that precious moment of here and now,
As heavenly bodies align in their celestial house,
The stars that glittered beyond the evening sky,
Flawless obiter for you, my ratio, a decision I made for
myself alone.
This I knew as I walked you home.

I did not think of tomorrow, I did not think of yesterday,
Because all I ever wanted was to have you hear me say,
"I love you, with all my heart and soul,"
Those fragile broken darkened bits of neglected self,
Temporarily made whole.
And you were patient, and you were kind,

But tonight was different as we did find,
All I said and did felt right,
As we stood beneath Osaka's moonlight.

At long last a moment shared,
To show you of all people how much I cared,
And for all the time that's already past I've always chosen
to remain steadfast.
If the ground should choose to quake,
Should typhoons threaten with howling bellow,
I'll prove it again, I'm an adamant fellow!
More so than any other you have met, I'll bet,
Win or lose this timeless gambit,
I'm not a man who can live with his regrets.

So maybe, just maybe, this crazy and unsustainable dream
leaves souvenirs of the most bittersweet kind. Or maybe,
just maybe, our modern fairy tale can write itself without
the crutch of 'happily ever after.'

While I gaze into the daze of your forget-me-not eyes,
Those precious gems have added pearls,
That validate the depth of emotions unfelt,
And I count myself blessed to have fallen for you,
For the fearlessness you inspire in me,
And all those new experiences I undertook,
To go beyond uncertainty,
And discover that in this life I would choose no other path
than the one that led us here tonight.
To be with you, and only you, in the ambience of Osaka
moonlight.

It is past midnight now, the magic starts to fade away.
We embrace goodbye, I inwardly sigh,
And for the first time since we've met,
This is the closest you've ever allowed me to get,
No walls nor similar distancing, that has always split me to my core.
We've bridged that gap with open honesty, unlike what we had before.
Unfairly we must part and exchange goodnights,
Though I confess, it took all my strength to walk away, and yes, I did look back...

My feelings are true feelings I've never once demanded you requite,
I was happiest when I could just be with you,
Illuminated by the Osaka moonlight.

"Miss Evergreen"

(For dearest Midori-chan, a penpal I *should* have met half a lifetime ago: we will always remember our Maple Story days. Also, in Chinese culture, jadestone is traditionally symbolic of virtue, vitality, and impeccable character. To compare one to jade can be seen as a high compliment which acknowledges one's positive impact on the world, while simultaneously wishing them great prosperity.)

In the city where angels reside,
A homage paid to all that is good and kind,
Embodies both beauty that never fades,
With character and zest one so rarely finds,
A dear friend truer than Emperor's Jades.

For my Jade Lady is not jaded, her vibrance evergreen!
For when distance is so desolate, that the gray frost sets,
I think of you, of our emerald past, adorning all that fickle
life begets,
Though your voice but a whisper, carried across the
winds,
Your form still spectral glimpse, waiting to be seen.

How I missed you, though I have never met you yet,

How I miss you still, for we are oceans and mountains
apart,
That I even miss missing you:
And all those times we bared our younger minds and
hearts.

I was 'Kappa,' hued as your namesake bid,
So very polite, behind eloquence hid,
You were as a big sister, my burdens became lightened,
If only for a moment: my weights were less heavy,
Your spirit nourished me from within.
For that, I will always be grateful.

Though oceans and mountains span between us, and times
flows forth, carries us separate ways,
I look forward to when we may share tea once again, for
the very first time....
To hear your wisdom and love of life, radiating from your
very being.
At such a time I can be sure that seeing is akin to
believing,
And our chance encounter will be time that has been well
spent.
Until that day, stay vibrant, Miss Evergreen!

"Earthbound Angel"

(For Angela, a true Queen. You have fed me on many occasions, nursed me in poor health, and chastised me as only a wise woman could.)

Should there be any doubts that you are too good to walk this earth unknowing,
Alay yourself self-doubting to what self-amounting you are worth.
For an angel who stays nought in Heaven, yet no less divine, resides instead on mortal Earth.

No greater joy exists than to meet a kindred soul,
Gladden amidst chance encounters yet to happen, along a lifetime's stroll.
In seeing how we click, I must admit, that we are family, if not by blood, then by your classic grace and charm and wit.

Were that all the leaves on every tree were tongues,
Alas how they still could not declare it!
How highly I value your esteem, they would be praising your character in vain...
For mere words alone could not express my fondness for your company.

Each syllable uttered to form speech spoken, a mere token
of that unique flair which puts all imitation to shame.

Surely you are an angel in human guise,
Wiser and more beautiful as time passes by.

The Gospel of Style

(Dedicated to my sister from another mister, Chantelle. Even though so much has changed over the years, you are the link that keeps us all connected, despite our busy lives.)

(Context: The following are about 3 suits I bought with my first paycheck, and grew to love. When it was time for a wardrobe update, I could not bear to dispose of them like common rags, instead opting to give each set of attire their own eulogy.)

"Seams 23: The tailor is my designer."

The tailor is my designer; I shall not want for style.
He maketh me to shine on magazine covers: he leadeth me beside the hipster culture.

He irons out my wrinkles: he leadeth me in the paths of fleek.
Yeah, though I catwalk through the Valley of the Shadow of Critics, I will fear no wardrobe malfunction: for artistic license is my soul; thy padding and thy pockets they do comfort me.

Thou preparest a photoshoot before me in the presence of
mine haters: thou anointest my threads with dry cleaning;
my classic look runneth over.

Surely to provide freshness for some homeless man, and a
vintage apparel shall follow me all the days of my display:
and I will hang fondly in the wardrobe of my tailor's
heart, always.

Take note of the lavender tie, complete with magenta lace finishings. The shirt's shade of pale sky blue allows for a wonderful overlay of softly contrasting colors, blended by the wearer's bold dark definition. The trousers were Asia-pop inspired, from a Singapore boutique, and travelled across Japan without a single zipper malfunction. The gray vest contributes and enhances the motif of sensible style, a signature of the owner's fashion sense of the pre-2010s era.

Thy tailor who art in manufacture,
Hallowed be thy seams.
Thy fashion come, thy style be done,
On the streets as it is in magazines.
Give us this day our daily selfie, and forgive us our
aesthetic choices, as we forgive those who dress-pas
against us.

Armani.

To the blazer from my Year 12 ball. For the longest time, I kept it, and now I'm giving it away. Perhaps the more speculative of you will say it represented a first love, the ante passage of a boy to a man. Or that it was the first suit I ever bought, so many years ago, when I dreamed of wearing a suit every day, one day. Regardless of what it meant, it holds such significance no longer, and the only value lies in its function, not nostalgia.

[I want to] Let the past fade away into the obscurity it belongs, to no longer dwell on feelings I preserved but instead to savor such experiences crafted anew. Only then will the choices we made have any real meaning.

"Links"

Ebony box,
Beholden within,
The gift of giving,
From words forgiven.

A timelessness to never forget,
Amidst our tapestry of joy and regrets.

Mother of pearl sheen partners the unfathomable black.

This is me as seen by my peers, the mystery of those
United lines, contrast as Arrows from 1989.

The bittersweet taste of our job well done is all I thought
to take back with me, but,

A bittersweet gift has yet to prove which is stronger over
time, the bitter, or the sweet.

The simplest way for us to communicate is to speak a
common language. Words do beget speech. Mistrust is their
suspicions, my sincerity is revealed by action. When they
are belligerent, I am forced to respond in kind. I have seen

the end, and it is fate that I will end you, yet we are not there yet; I would show you kindness before I take your life.

"The Lonely God"

It hurts me,
To experience different timelines.
We are friends in one,
Strangers in another.
I see what you cannot remember,
My existential angst.

I create myself, so I can never forget,
But you are self-creating,
A cause for such envy you could never understand.
So I am left with such regrets,
That our tenuous relationship is doomed from the start.
For any canvas that paints itself requires no artist's brush.

My desire to be closer,
Your fierce independence,
Perhaps we are defined by that distance.
Maybe one day it will mend, this cycle could end.

Until that time, I shall remain a lonely god.

"Not Yes"

Strictly speaking, I am a businessman,
And all my choices reflect that creed,
A safe secure investment is all I'll ever need.
Yet what worthwhile gains avail themselves to a man who
takes no risk?
So I extend an offer of mutual growth-
You need only sign it with a kiss.
A fever most fervent,
Excitement runneth over,
Anticipates the rise in stock of such a company merger.
In good health and prosperity,
Awaiting a final answer:
Yet to arrive.
A silence that prompts my inner wonder, if I had
overstepped my bounds?
As frantic overtakes the prior calm,
Until at last, the truth, sweet 'n' sour, blossoms, clear and
true,
That dream I seek to start and build is not the same for
you... I sought to mix my business with leisure,
mistaken what I thought we felt amidst the social
pleasures.
Thus I've violated a most golden rule,

Guilty of a most professional sin.
That is when the realization settles in,
"Not yes," is answer clear enough,
To accept what a fool I've been.
As ship sets sails and I'm left behind,
I must also accept with better grace,

There are no profits here for me to find,
It's unbecoming of my corporate face,
Leaves me no room for private affection.
I am but a lonely businessman, making money, not
connections.
Please know, I think it was worth the taken chance,
To build something rivaled by so few!
I would never regret what was said and done, nor what I
felt for you.
Always grateful for how you've helped me change and
grow.
Nonetheless...
'Not No' may not be the same as 'Yes,'
'Not Yes' is plainly 'no.'

Her Name Was V

(Even if this wasn't her real name, I daresay she and I shared
a special relationship that was only partly fueled by money)

'Twas not the ample sway,
Of your buxom bosom, bountiful as the harvest goddess,
Not those supple, lithe limbs that invite my gaze, and
subsequent dexterous address,
Your face reminisce of marble art, sculpted, so striking
and refined.
Nor was it that graceful tongue that spoke caressing words
with unabashed embrace.
Even as your scent lingers amongst my formal attire,
That soulfulness you've stirred within,
Is as free and welcoming as those windows to your soul.
Your lovely eyes peer into thine,
And express the woman you are,
Beautiful inside, as well as out.
Were that minutes became hours as we play our coyish
game,

"How many summers have we seen?"
"From which and whence from my hearth did sprung?"
"Are you as genuine in body as you are in soul?"

Answers mattered not,
And paled when compared,
To what you spoke without the need for words.
Your zest for life, the fire of adventure burns bright,
springs forth!
Catching me ablaze, my entrancement amidst those
flames.
Each breathe fills me with your very essence; witful and
charming, you show modesty still,

"Merely eau de parfume, Chanel Madamoiselle,"

To which I reply, "A painting is more than just the colors
of an artist's palette."

And when the time comes that you've bared yourself
completely to me,
I understand what kind of secrets lie between us,
None pertinent in our moment of sincerity,
Complements well our synergy,
As we must say goodnight, while promising to meet again.
Your name to me, while a mystery,
Evermore my V, for Verity

"My Quantum Valentine"

(Dedicated to all who think of dating as 'too hard')

Alone, not lonely,
As I wander through the quiet streets.
My soul unburdened by ennui,
I drift not for melancholy, yet it was not for naught that I
discovered it. – Kataware Doki

If our existence is the unknowable state, at that moment I
could be certain.
Calm still air blankets the entire field, as far as eye could
see,
Perhaps as if to preserve, that beacon which called me
forth, with unwitting intent, to witness a chance splendor
as fleeting as is unforgettable,
Double rainbow at twilight!
Although this place, not devoid of people strolling at their
leisurely pace,
All of us felt connected by heavenly joy that isolates from
each party present.
I think to myself, how lovely it would be,
Walking hand-in-hand with a certain fair lady,
As we embrace a single, timeless, moment, seemingly
unbound by time and space...

As transient as life may be, that would be enough for me.
Or so I would like to believe, as the skies darkened over
this place now vacant lot, Empty, except for me.

As I gaze into the evening nebula, my soul still reliving
moments ago,
Warm rains begin to fall, as if my solitude has moved the
heavens to tears,
Celestial weeping now clears the air, and somewhat
begins to part the clouds.

I can see the moon, shining through,
Amidst a backdrop of midnight blue,
And although I know that starry companions do
accompany their umbral peer,
At present all I can see is the moon, like myself, not lonely,
nonetheless alone.

Now at last I understand,
That serendipity which drew me here,
As I stand drenched with rain,
And the evening's mood starts to chill,
Only to have borne witness to this cosmic lesson in love.

"Dangerous Games"

A debt of blood demands repayment in blood.
A society that denies dreams will be forced to become a
living nightmare.
The future is a peculiar thing, for what I do today decides
what I awaken to tomorrow.
Forgive me, Odysseus, I could not resist partaking of the
divine flock.

Don't you know?
The Royal Flush is but a straight flush putting on airs.
There is no true difference in our hands,
For we both play to win.

A guessing game is played,
To better understand each other.
Asking questions,
Answering in turn,
"Is there someone else?" you ask,
I would not lie to someone I love
So I choose to omit.
"Isn't that the same thing" you ask,
I cannot lie to someone I love.
"Do you love me?"

The heart has many reasons for doing what it does, that
Reason alone can never fathom.

I'm in love with the mystery, the chase, the hunt.
The object of my affection is a mere convenience.
To lavish, to serenade, and praise.
I am not the dark, I am a shadow.
There is so much power in my feelings,
Tremendous energy trapped within my thoughts,

For you are the light that drives me and gives me shape,
Your light will destroy me if we ever embraced.

"Farewells"

Ephemeral shooting star at 9:39
Your beauty rests not on thy destiny to fade,
But in the audience that witness your fleeting whisper:
"Forget me not."

He uses her without a second thought,
But she does not mind being used.
She does not question why,
His sins she takes upon herself.
For it is for one and one purpose alone that she like all the
rest of her kind exist,
Only duty; she receives nothing in return
When all is said and done,
A used napkin receives a last kiss goodbye.

"0448328816"

Have any mortal eyes yet divined?
Such beauty in this sequence of mine!
Not since Fibonacci have I felt such bliss,
To express these numbers by each lipless kiss.

Consider the origin of all things, its introductory figure.
Creatio ex Nihilo, that miracle which denies not God.
Which holds space with such humble vigor,
Then those twins that follow true,
Forming perfect union to honor you.
For 7 the so called prime that seals one's fate,
Yet 7 so selfish, in self-loving and hate.
My Venus of clear, superior, veneer,
She is my one and only 8.
Unlike the others so shallow, possessing greatest depth.
In 3 dimensions a pairing results,
What is better than one, than to double one's fun?
The perfect pairs unite,
As I recall being sweet 16 once again.
Filled with sudden tender first love at first sight,
Deepened by a second glance.

"Mr. East Rivers"

(For Will, a steadfast companion of buffets and good conversation, always be welcome at my table: any meal shared with you always tastes better.)

If I lived until 100,
I'd still never be as cool as you,
Oh, Mr. East Rivers!

A smart-alec grin sans the chagrin,
Your warmth and caring, on the inside,
Adds depth to fun-jesting,
So witty, so snide!
With you I have no reason to mask or hide,
And yet I still do,
Because you enjoy masquerades too!

If I made a billion dollars,
Gained a million fans,
You'd still be more popular, the richer man!
Oh, Mr. East Rivers!

In good times we shared bounty and joy,
When those times soured, you didn't leave my side,

In sorrow we find out I'm not easily toyed,
I patiently wait, time was mine to bide.
Until it came time for that grand reveal.
No matter how distant I seemed,
You remain my true friend in my time of need,
A peer who lightens my burdens,
Your soul brings song to my silence,
A man whose company I treasure dear.

Please never cease sharing your wonderful self,
Especially when you make it a more wonderful world,
Mr. East Rivers.

"The Flavor of Nostalgic Tea"

(For my kind LaoShu mei-mei, who put up with my
random antics, and always showed me that no matter how
good we think we are to others, there's always someone
doing more.)

As evening settles, I fancy a brew,
Of tea leaves hoarded, now long past due.
Yet the feelings evoked is my calling, to drink a cup filled
with quiet memories.
To taste a blend of tastebud melodies,
Playing for me a wistful tune of simpler times.
A simple flavor I've since forgotten, from a time when I
didst used to care,
Faded leaves bathing away the dust, simmering in boiled
and gentle despair.

A vessel of clay to temper the heat,
And 30 seconds later, a fragrant hue,
Stream of dark river pours into my cup,
As I ponder my search for limbic cues.

Was it always destined to turn out this way?

I take my first sip, shy suitor with awkward lips, who dares
a small peck and soon finds himself
indulging deeper and deeper, to discover such flavors that
his embraced supplies.

This is a tea that has waited 5 years, or more?
Yet such deepness evoked from my patient neglect, and
causes me to sit, and reflect.

That I've not squandered my time, yet to pass me by,
That I ought do more than sip tea with battle weary sigh.

That I should savor the taste of a vintage brew,
That beckons to my past self I've yet proved untrue.

"Climate Change"

The Heat you prefer, I'd rather the Cold.
Not that I don't enjoy the heat, for warmth is that blessing
known to newborn babes.
With it, I am content, happy, and feel safe.
Except, I am never sure of the latter.

The Cold? Yes, a bitter mistress, but it keeps my mind
sharp, it numbs the pain, and reminds me to be strong.
I've known no other love since I can remember, so much
so that I now **am** the frost, the ice, the snow.
Cooling my urge for company, freezing the weakness of
needing to belong.

My strength lies in my solitude.

Thusly, in your embrace, I am afraid; that I'd melt away,
and I would not know who I am any more.
But I would chance to spend the Summers with you, that
my ever Winter may become the Spring.

The Poet Tree

"Never withers, ever blooming,
My fruit my namesake, plain to see.
Always elegant, oh so eloquent,
I am a poet tree!"

There was a time when I had some poignant feels for a girl, and after some hesitation, I decided to express them by literally crafting my sentiments. I made an ornament, a rather simple little bonsai-esque tree, which featured origami roses (modelled after the Kawasaki flower style). Each flower contained a poem I had composed specifically for her, to stand as testament to my affections. She was a friend who I had grown very fond of, and I was wary of any romantic potential as I valued our previously uncomplicated relationship. The design has a few deliberate features that flirts with romance conventions, mainly revolving around the fact that the origami roses offered poems that could not be read unless one 'plucked' the flower, which represented a teasing mystery. Another thing to note, which is less profound, is the wordplay involved – a Poet Tree that produces poetry? Surely this is proof that my sense of humor has ascended the mortal realm. Regardless of whether or not she returned my feelings, I felt that my own emotions were a beautiful phenomenon that did not require outside validation. I took what I felt for her was a sign that I had learned enough to love myself again. Eight poems were composed for the tree, but have revealed only six of them here – after all, it was a gift meant solely for her, and the two that remain solely hers were shaped from my most authentic, clumsy feelings, which I would prefer to remain between us.

1. Although slyly you shy away from me,
Conceal that self that resides deep inside,
A painted face not for face but soul,
That hidden self that makes you whole.
If by means of showing strength you would discard that tender side,
If by me you would not contain, and instead choose to hide,
Then by all means I would comply to such whimsy,
Accede to faux countenance so flimsy,
As to deny how lovely you are from your maidenly score.
I glimpse that special hidden truth, endures forever more.

2. When I hear your voice,
It is not the sound of angels singing,
Yet no less musical to my ears.
Would you have not, or prefer to have – then a loss,
For words I am become as a stranger longs for a familiar face.
In you I am blessed to have one so fair to view,
In you, there lies a gentle mirth to comfort my parched soul.
It is experience thine, that celestial beings care not for me,

And the divine hides coldness for those unfortunates as I.
So when I hear your voice, it be not the sound of angels
singing,
Your words carry far more meaning: they carry me from
my despair.
Your laughter stirs from mine somber moods, akin to
breathing fresh air.

3. Could it be we are the impossible?
What, then what, do we ascertain?
A Grimm pairing of the fox and wolf,
As akin to the frog and scorpion.
Were such parables indeed gospel proven true,
Then, what then, becomes of me and you?
There are no bees without flowers,
Nor are there flowers without bees.
When nature's partnerships are struck,
Tis a deal done, an arrangement for life.
So happy we agree to follow the spree,
Thus let us continue to run amok!

4. Do you recall those times when you and I,
Picnicked with each, nit-picked one another,
From azure pure blue to starry night sky.
You don't? Neither do I.
Remembered when the winter set in,
And it was just the two of us inside our cozy den.
A hot drink for you, a cooler one for me,
Sipping between the games we played,
While winds played games among the rustling leaves,
I maintain I won most games,

Because the true winner was always me,
Enjoying myself by your side.

5. Hot days encourage not the best in me,
Much less enclosed in my coffinesque space,
My parched mouth sopped by what remains of an earlier
swig,
That only serves to remind me what I have not.
Thus I sink into a sullen resentful mood, unsmiling and
sore.
Perhaps like this all day I would've remained,
Until a cool breeze dissolves the unborn hate,
That p'haps didst resides within my unsatisfied heart.
And I am grateful for all the simple pleasures of life.
Whenever I wonder if this world serves as naught but my
bane,
I need only think of you,
Were that I had naught else in this desert,
A mere sip of water may as well be an oasis,
It is enough for me.

6. You astound me as no one can,
At times awkward, at times clumsy,
Yet never awkwardly nor clumsily so.
I find it irresistible,
To witness your mock outrage,
When things don't go your way,
As if to say,
"How dare they?!"
So undeniably, irresistibly, unfathomably-
Charming.

In a way your guardedness rarely allows to show.
And it would be a shame if no one saw it.
If no one else could see it to believe it/
Aren't you most fortunate then,
To have me, your ever attentive friend?

"Loose Ends"

"What's more apt,
When at the end?
Eulogy too solemn,
A Swan Song then.
For just a friend,
From just a friend.
For the first time, and the last,
I understand past romance lost.
I was but a boy, learning to be a man.
Now I truly comprehend:
Mature Love, not bitter, though may leave traces bitter-
sweet.
It is not hopeless, yet too jaded to hope.
I do not utter those words,
Yet my gestures do not suffice,
To convey how deeply and sincere,
That I have loved you for some time.
Yet, now, I have to love myself,
Still learning, a novice, true.
Yet I can't afford to be hurt again,
Without resenting you.
Rather than the natural course,
Or denying what I feel.

I will choose to let it go,
And become something else more real.
Not all the tales end with ever after,
But it was a fairytale, nonetheless,
Amongst the girls who have come and gone,
You were the one who I loved best.
My healthiest attraction, my final test.
Perhaps it would have been worthwhile,
And then again, mayhaps we avoided catastrophe!

That Games of Hearts seems so trivial now.
And I am lucid beyond all words.
Never regretting the time we spent,
But I'll cut my losses, buff out these dents,
So that one day we can once again walk side by side,
uncompromised, no need to lie to spare feelings that would
do better to not feel.
Let's settle matters, tie loose ends, and give us both some
time to heal.
For a friend, from just a friend-
The End."

"Just Laugh:
A Nebulous Eulogy"

*Epitaph: He solemnly swore to live a solo man's life,
enshrouded by loneliness that had nothing to do with a
lack of company.*

*There can be no truer way than one chosen by my own
hand,
For this is the end I chose,
Not the one that life or fate or circumstance deemed fit to
bestow.*

*Return the razor which has no intention to shave,
An untaut rope is hanging loose without a noose.
Still, finality approaches, and I accept the outcome with
open arms.*

*In so many ways I kept the faith, my solitude ungrim,
Accepted 'love' upon a whim.*

*There is strength in solitude, and I was very strong.
My way of living could not afford to be wrong.*

Intoxicating frivolities arise from joy seeking,

Could not keep pace with emotions I was keeping,
Contained within a beating chest, locked away, that I may
know rest.
For what I craved was peace, not love or faith or
happiness.

And in my desolate kingdom I slept, undisturbed by what
lay beyond the uncertain horizon.
Until I awoke to find myself, now older and more able,
Mind and heart surprisingly stable.
And I discovered that in my slumber I had grown a soul.

What is a soul, if such things do exist?
Which I know they do, for I have one now.
To understand, I think, the things I knew before,
I do not suffer as a lonely man, anymore.

I wonder, and am comforted by newfound awareness.
"You mistook knowledge for wisdom, and used force in
lieu of strength.
That is why you were not powerful, yet far from weak.
Lacking in naught except belief, and thus became a nihilist
of extraordinary empathy"

Ah, it is so clear to me now.
A grin of sardonic enlightenment.

What I tried to control was merely an illusion of my self-
importance,
To love and be loved is to employ courageous strength,
rather than a despairing one.

A frog looking for a princess to help him become a prince,
As a king he may treat her as she deserves: a queen.

My empty heart was the illusion of inner peace,
Shattered by the turbulence of being human,
A calm heart is the reality of being.

I did not choose to fall in love,
But I chose to stay once I fell,
And I am open to growing.
Exploring what I started knowing,
Having come back from that private hell.

Faith requires mystery to prove itself, vindicated,
Accept the unknown with an open heart.
After everything that has happened,
I can only laugh!

CPSIA information can be obtained
at www.ICGtesting.com
Printed in the USA
LVHW081222310523
748422LV00009B/101

9 781647 505462